INTRODUCTION

GOSSIP GIRL IS WRITTEN TO INSPIRE WOMEN OF ALL AGES AS ENCOURAGEMENT TO INSPIRE THEM TO FIND THEIR PURPOSE IN CHRIST; AND TO EFFECTIVELY LIVE OUT THEIR LIVES KNOWING THAT CIRCUMSTANCES AND ISSUES WILL ARISE: BUT THROUGH A CONSISTENT AND STRATEGIC PRAYER LIFE, THEIR FAITH AND TRUST IN GOD, THEY CAN BE KEPT BY GODS SUSTAINING POWER. GODS DIVINE Plan and Gods unfailing love. I wrote this to share with women that every set back; rejection and pain that I have endured has helped catapult me into this very moment. His will not ours is the perfect secret to being kept. Its all our relationship with the creator.

Table of Contents

CHAPTER 1: NO MORE BROKEN MIRRORS

GENESIS 1:26-27 KJV AND GOD SAID LET US MAKE MAN IN OUR IMAGE AFTER OUR LIKENESS AND LET THEM HAVE DOMINION OVER THE FISH OF THE SEA AND OVER THE FOWL OF THE AIR AND OVER THE CATTLE AND OVER THE EARTH AND OVER EVERY CREEPING THING THAT CREEPETH UPON THE EARTH. SO, GOD CREATED MAN IN HIS OWN IMAGE IN THE IMAGE OF GOD CREATED HE THEM.MY DEAR SISTER WHAT ARE YOU SEEING WHEN YOU LOOK IN THE MIRROR? GODS INTENTION FROM THE BEGINNING WAS you are TO RECOGNIZE THAT you ARE BEAUTIFUL FEARFULLY AND WONDERFULLY MADE. REGARDLESS OF ANY FLAWS, GODS DESIGN FOR YOU WAS TO COME

INTO THE KNOWLEDGE THAT YOU ARE LIKE HIM;

NOT HIM BUT LIKE HIM you HAVE HIS DNA HIS

DESIGN. THE ENEMY PLAN IS TO KEEP you

BOUND IN AN IDENTITY crisis THAT IS NOT OF

GOD TO KEEP you SHACKLED IN your MIND AND

IN your THOUGHT PROCESSES THAT WILL HAVE

you THINK THA you ARE BLEMISHED AND

DISFIGURED HE WANTS you NOT TO SEE Yourself

AS GOD SAYS you ARE. SATANS INTENTIONS ARE

THAT WHEN you LOOK IN MIRRORS THAT you

RECOGNIZE MEER IMAGES OF your SCARS; OF

BROKENESS, of UNHEALED OPEN WOUNDS

AND DISFIGURATIONS OF HIS LIES OF LIFES

CIRCUMSTANCES AND ISSUES THAT have

CAUSED you TO NOT SEE yourself AS THE DIVINE

MASTERPIECES THAT you ARE. When Your

HEAVENLY FATHER GAVE HIS ONLY BEGOTTEN

SONS LIFE AS A RANSOM FOR you SO THAT you

MAY HAVE LIFE MY SISTERS it was in THAT pivotal moment THAT TRIUMPHED OVER EVERY SCHEME OF THE ENEMY. JOHN 3:16 KJV FOR GOD SO LOVED THE WORLD THAT HE GAVE HIS ONLY BEGOTTEN SON THAT WHOSOEVER BELIEVETH IN HIM SHOULD NOT PERISH BUT HAVE EVERLASTING LIFE. SO THAT IS WHY I ENCOURAGE YOU TO RECOGNIZE DAILY YOUR PURE ESSENCE OF BEAUTY WRAPPED UP IN GODS LOVE OF COURSE WE ALL HAVE FLAWS BUT GOD LOVES US REGARDLESS OF THEM. SATANS PLAN IS TO KEEP you BOUND BUT GODS PLAN IS THAT you WALK LIBERATED. GOD HAS A PURPOSE AND PLAN FOR your Life .MY SISTERS WHEN THINGS CHANGE ON THE INSIDE OF YOU THEN THINGS WILL BEGIN TO CHANGE AROUND YOU. EVEN in THE MOST BROKEN POINTS IN your Life WHAT THE BROKEN MIRROR REVEALS IS

GODS LOVE FOR you. Your only requirement is that you HAVE TO BE WILLING TO accept GODS LOVE for you WHICH IS THE LIGHT THAT RESTORES you. THE BROKEN MIRROR IS you NOW, you ARE THE MIRROR IN ITS ENTIRETY WHOLE OR BROKEN IT IS you HOWEVER THOUGH THANK GOD FOR HIS SOVERIEGN GRACE AND FOR HIS tender mercies BECAUSE AS you BEGIN TO EMBRACE GOD, THE BROKENENESS BECOMES BEAUTIFUL IF you SURRENDER your ALL TO HIM AND HIS WILL FOR your Life. HIS PURPOSE NOT your OWNS. You Must not ALLOW ANYTHING TO HINDER you FROM SEEING your REFLECTION you MUST OFTEN LOOK AT yourself AND TRULY SEE WHAT you HAVE BECOME AS A PERSON IN DOING THAT you MUST NOT BE DECIEVED BY SATAN AND NOT ALLOW THE WHISPERS OF HIS LIES AND

DECEPTION TO DICTATE to you who you and who you are not , nor whom God has called you to become. you MUST BE CONFIDENT in CHRIST. IT IS THE HOLY SPIRIT THAT REPAIRS you THROUGH you FAITH IN CHRIST.SIN HAS CAUSED your BROKEN MIRRORS BUT all praises TO GOD BECAUSE THROUGH THE DEATH BURIAL AND RESURRECTION OF JESUS CHRIST THERE IS TRANSFORMING POWER THAT will begin your PROCESS of restoration ALLOWING CHRIST TO MAKE you WHOLE AGAIN. Ladies you serve a God that supersedes your expectations REMEMBER SATAN JOB IS TO KILL STEAL AND DESTROY; BUT REMEMBER THAT God created you to beautiful masterpieces that reflect Him.

CHAPTER 2 THE RIGHT STRUT SISTERS

2 CORINTHIANS 5;7 KJV FOR WE WALK BY FAITH AND NOT BY SIGHT. SO, I KNOW THAT AS WOMEN WE ALL LOVE TO HAVE A GOOD Strut and STRIDE, that signature walk. SO, MY QUESTION IS HOW ARE YOU REALLY WALKING.IT IS IMPORTANT THAT AS WOMEN OF FAITH you HAVE THE RIGHT PERCEPTIVE ABOUT WHAT DOES WALKING BY FAITH NOT BY SIGHT MEAN. WALKING BY FAITH Not BY SIGHT MEANS ALTHOUGH you MAY NOT SEE God in your circumstances right now, you must trust that he

is preparing you for blessings and relief from what you are facing somewhere down the road. See as women of faith you must never forget that Gods' presence is always with you, although you may have issues; and yes, life will continue to life but as long as you walk in the confidence and boldness believing that nothing catches God by surprise; that God is all seeing and all-knowing. As a woman, sisters we you may even venture off course by the wayside or have some valley experiences but do not stop walking and pressing your way through them because remember Gods presence is in those low places with you. I promise if you walk knowing that God is in control your, God will shift those detours and reroute you, Girl often into a better position than before. God's word promises that he will always make a way for you through everything. God will cause mountains to move and every wall in your life to fall with his power nothing that there is nothing impossible for God. Remember that God is always by your side. You must remember to continually ACCEPT, CONFESS AND ACKNOWLEDGE THAT you NEED JESUS!!

FIVE WAYS TO ENRICH YOUR DAILY WALK WITH GOD:

1. START AND END EVERY DAY WITH GOD WITH THANKSGIVING AND PRAYER
2. KNOW THAT WHAT IS AND ISNT IMPORTANR
3. PLACE SPIRITUAL BOUNDARIES IN YOUR LIFE
4. READ AND MEDITATE ON SCRIPTURE
5. REMEMBER THAT YOU ARE FEARFULLY AND WONDERFULLY MADE.

You MUST KNOW THAT EACH DAY AS WE you

THIS FAITH WALK, THAT GOD LOVES you EVEN

THOUGH you ARE IMPERFECT AND STILL

PROGRESSING TO BE BETTER. In life you will

encounter some delays but remember that a

delay when you are in covenant with God is never

a denial it is merely a divine delay and that

oftentimes setbacks are set up by the enemy; and

even so know the God you serve will take that

same pitstop and make it work for your good. It is

in that moment when you are walking this thing

out call life that GOD comes to RESCUE YOU.

YOUR HELP IS ON THE WAY DON'T YOU GIVE UP

JUST CALL ON JESUS AND WATCH HE COME SEE

ABOUT YOU RIGHT NOW RIGHT THERE IN THE

MIDDLE OF IT. SISTERS HURDLES ARE NOT STOP

SIGNS; keep walking by faith and not by your

sight. In the year 2007 I needed prayer,

determination and the right encouragement after my marriage was attacked and I went through a divorce. I was devastated; God carried me through my pain disappointment and my shame and the guilt that was I feeling. I was having a battle in my mind, but God reminded me on the days that I wanted to give up that He was still able to help me make it. Even in my doubt God continued to remind me that He was still able. My sister you must know that that God is able he has not changed and that he will order your steps. BABY GOD TOOK THAT DIVORCE AND TURNED IT INTO MY DELIVERENCE; MY GOD IN HEAVEN, I LOVE YOU JESUS.... GOD IS A HEALER SISTERS... GOD HEALED ME AS THE HOLY SPIRIT GAVE ME COMFORT AND I FOUND PEACE AND REST. IM STILL VALUED I STILL HAVE PURPOSE INSPITE OF THE DIVORCE. GOD REMINED ME THAT IM HIS

DAUGHTER HIS GEM A WOMEN WHO WALKS IN
PURPOSE DOES NOT HAVE TO CHASE PEOPLE
OR OPPORTUNITIES; THAT HE WILL CAUSE HIS
FACE TO SHINE UPON ME AND THE RIGHT
RELATIONSHIP WILL PURSUE ME AT HIS
APPOINTED TIME. TWENTY YEARS LATER MY EX-
HUSBAND AND I ARE FRIENDS WE HAVE
MANAGED TO CO-PARENT IN A HEALTHY WAY.
FORGIVENESS IS LIBERATING YALL. ITS IN THAT
MOMENT WHEN GOD HEARD MY CRY; God
wants us. WHEN I decided to LET GO AND
ALLOWED GOD TO MAKE ME WHOLE, I REALIZED
THAT GOD WAS EVERTHING THAT I NEEDED TO
GET ME THROUGH. I HAVE EXPECTATIONS OF
THE MANIFESTATIONS OF MY NEW Husband God
positioned   me in this season from wanting to
WAITING... Despite failures sisters remember
that you are born to rise if you; even if you are

walking alone, you are not alone you can make it.

Girl you are unstoppable when you are walking in

your God given purpose; nothing cannot stop

Gods purpose for you. God created you for His

reason and that reason is His divine purpose and

assignment for your life. The most important

healing process through my divorce was learning

that finding purpose was a universal heart cry

fulfilling your purpose and walking in your

purpose gives God the glory and release you from

the captivity of hopelessness and despair. Okay I

know you are probably saying Girl what are you

talking about, well check this out the bible says

forgetting what is behind and striving toward what

is ahead I press on toward the goal to win the

prize which God has called me heavenward in

Christ Jesus(philippians3:13-14). I had to put my

anger, my regret my bitterness and my pain

behind me before I could focus on the race God had set before me. I had to hear Gods voice over the noise and confusion in which I lived. God wants you to heed the apostle Paul's counsel. Since we live by the spirit let us keep in step with the spirit (Galatians 5:25). The holy spirit will lead you. I love the way God takes a willing EARTHEN VESSEL no matter how broken or scarred her past may be and weaves every intricate thread of her life into his kingdom plan. He does not shy away from hurts and failures but specializes in hope, in second chances and in resurrections. Girl I never imagined my tough experiences would give me the substance I now need to minister to others; I had no idea that God was preparing me through my divorce deliverance to offer the same hope to other women. my sisters I encourage you to hang onto the hope that God does have a plan for life as the bible promises in Jeremiah 29:11 for I know the plans I have for you, declares the lord plans to prosper you and not to harm you plans to give you hope and a future; you will make it through. SO, WALK IT OUT SISTERS BY FAITH....

CHAPTER 3 BIZARRELY BLESSED

GOD, I GIVE YOU PRAISE FOR ALL YOU HAVE DONE. I did not understand why things happened to me, things would be going great: I had all this favor, but how to manage when conflict and struggle still shows up. Oftentimes God will let you feel uncomfortable now so that he can bless you later. God closes doors you, oftentimes you do not understand. You may not like it; but trust that God will open a bigger, door he will get you to new levels, and new destinations. TRUST THE

PROCESS through the uncomfortable season

God wants you to rest in him through the storm.

God is not as concerned about your comfort as

He is your purpose. Girl there is often instances

when God will stir things it up in your life it may

show up as a friend that does you wrong, family

problems, issues on the job. Nothing catches

God by surprise. God uses what you may see as

loss, or betrayal, or persecution to catapult you to

change. GOD is not making your life miserable He

is merely pushing you into your purpose; besides

I'm sure you can think of a lot of wrong places you

could be without Him; every closed door is not a

bad thing all failed relationships are not mistakes;

God knows what He really need to work for your

good; so often he just shakes things loose. Girl,

you know you are trying to hold on to stuff that is

no good for you or good to you... GOD, I

PERSONALLY THANK YOU FOR SHAKING SOME THINGS LOOSE OFF ME. God knows when you need that push, thank you Jesus for the assistance of the Holy SPIRIT. When things are comfortable, you are good and the times even when things are not comfortable the enemy tries to keep you bound by thinking you are good in that foolery girl you best get out that trauma. What was held up is now being released in this season. Speak Jesus today, Girl you better let God get some stuff done for you without you, all you need to do is obey and some stuff will come up on its on for you; the right divine connections, God ordained sister- friends, God purposed skills. If you want to experience the bizarrely blessings of GOD, you must seek purpose, it is time for a change sister. God closed doors that He knew were not beneficial for you in that season. God loves you so much that by any means necessary He will not let you miss his distinguished destiny he has prepared for you. God will put you in situations that force you to stretch, that will help you to grow and glow through every difficult situation that you have been through every bad break has not been meant to break you, I found that those issues are meant to mature you to make you stronger. God uses difficulties to deposit substance on the inside of you; God deposits this thing called STRENGHT; WHICH HAS BEEN A DEFINING FACTOR IN WHO YOU ARE TODAY. As I look back over my life, I can see the pivotal moments where I really stepped up to new level. The common denominator, it was God pushed me, I did not like it, I was uncomfortable right there in my mess. It took God closing doors forcing me to take a step of faith , I was pushed into my purpose sometimes you may praying against the very thing God has ordained or set in motion to bless you, the enemy doesn't close every door; God closes doors, God causes things to dry up to force you to change, to quit being depressed over that somebody that walked away from you if they left your life their time was up step up into your new season. If the door closed, you went through a disappointment, do not complain you are about to walk into your purpose: you are about to see new growth, new opportunities, and new friendships. In scripture, the prophet Samuel spent years pouring into king Saul, he had mentored him as a young man loved him like his own son but unfortunately; Saul would not do what was right. 1 Samuel 16:11(NIV)the lord said to Samuel how long will you mourn for Saul since I have rejected him as king over Israel fill your horn with oil and be on your way God has new levels ,more favor ,more influence ,more resources his dream for your life IS bigger than you can imagine every time major growth PRESENTS IT SELF every time God allows YOU to elevate there will be opposition adversity challenges and maybe some loss. You may be in a situation right now you could easily be discouraged you may have lost a loved a one although the enemy may have meant it for your bad, but God is going to use that very situation for your good God will not allow anything that the Satan intended to break you be in vain. God will not allow ANYTHING to hinder his divine plan for your life., Girl that very thing was only a push to propel you into your set purpose. God allowed the push, remember Job; and just like Job you are going to come out wiser stronger healthier increased and better off than you were before. Be encouraged that God is taking YOU into another place in him regardless of YOUR scars, your blemishes and even those bruises, God will use it all for your good and his glory. Perhaps you have been betrayed sis that same betrayal will make you seek God for better relationships, into new happiness the pain is a sign that you are about to see a birthing, remember the greater the difficulty the closer you are to your breakthrough, God often uses the very thing that you see as an irritant position you. Baby you best believe Gods word that he will use your enemies to be your footstools; while they were trying to sabotage your character, that very assault was used to get you to your already secured victory, so please just stay in the race, sis go through it, grow through it, because you are close to it. Judas thought that when he betrayed Jesus, he was stopping Him. But the truth of the matter is that He was part of Gods divine plan to promoting Jesus to the ultimate victory that would save a wretch like you and me. Remember my sisters to trust God through all things. It is a new day keep the right perspective. Four years ago, I lost my son Trent Matthew Jones "JETT," a victim to gun violence at the age of eighteen he was a senior in high school at the time of his death. I never expected to bury one of my children so soon; but even in my child's transitioning I still say that the blessings of God make you rich and add no sorrow. Some may ask the question as to why or may be wondering why I say I'm bizarrely blessed the enemy used the death of my child as a plot, he thought it would cause me to lose my mind; he thought it would shake my faith in God, he thought it would make me lose my praise and trust in God. All I can say is that it is indescribable; God took the one thing that the adversary used to break me, God turned it around and has used it to bless me and my children immensely we are closer we are stronger and wiser. We love different. I raised my children up in the admonition of God all five of them. Romans 8:28 says, and we know that all things work for the good of those who love him who have been called according to his purpose. God uses all things, including the difficulties of life to refine people's faith, strengthen their endurance, and develop their character. God has remained faithful to me even in the passing of my baby boy, God blessed me, God can redeem anything, even difficult things for His honor. I love my baby and I miss Him but rest on the promises of God and the peace that God provides to me. God promised me and my children that there is Life after death and that he would continue to bless us and carry us through our new norm. Yes you can, God with his strategic self has carried me through from my baby boys alpha to his omega and he is carrying me in this very moment as my comforter as He fulfills this very assignment through me, God spoke to me when Trent was the tender age of fourteen that He was a Prophet and that He would use that child to take me around the world; I thought the he meant my boy would be playing professional basketball because my boy was gifted and talented with that basketball he would soar on that basketball court just like a JETT, who knew that God promise is still being fulfilled because I get to witness, minister and encourage and inspire communities and families of survivors that if they stand on the promises of God's word through their pain that God will still allow them to Have Life after the death of their loved ones; and to walk I often pray that families that have lost family members to violence get to the point that the can walk in true forgiveness because it is a part of living in peace of God. Yes, you can make it, yes you can. No, you do not have to succumb to the tactics of Satan, you will not be depressed and stay grief stricken you will smile and remember to joy your loved one filled your life with every moment. Every set back, every tear I have cried and will cry of hope, can never compare to the comfort and peace of mind that I am feeling right now knowing that Holy Spirit is comforting me right now as I pen this assignment and I know that my Boy is smiling down on me even now. FLY HIGH JETT TAKE YOUR REST MOMMY LOVES YOU UNTIL ETERNITY... FOREVER

Chapter 4 Declaration of Independence

We must remember in our spirit that we are

perfect children of God that is why Paul said

when we remove the veil (our mask) from our

faces we can understand the glory of Christ that

is with us. 2 Corinthians 3:18 and we all with

unveiled face beholding the glory of the lord

being: transformed into the same image from one

degree of glory to another for this comes from the

lord who is the spirit. So, all of you who have the

veil removed can see and reflect the glory of the

lord. The more you look to Jesus the more you will

show the characteristics of Jesus. Ladies it is

time to take the mask off and to allow the holy ghost of God open your eyes to see the glory of Jesus the beauty the wonder the love the truth the majesty of Jesus peace. You must have unveiled faces life's issues can sometimes incapacitate you, by keeping you in old shame or hurt, scars, abuse, abandonment, and abuse and not feeling loved; but I encourage you today to grab a hold of Gods peace. BUT GOD! Today I encourage you to receive that there is absolutely no reason to remain masked up in any area of your life .my sisters take them mask off; sister-friend you are free release the shame and the guilt today. God has made you fierce whole, holy, unblemished, faithful, shameless, and radiant. So that is why it is imperative to put the enemies' scheme to shame and take the mask off. Because John 8:36 if the son sets you free you will be free indeed the woman who struggle with the shame from her past or present is not walking in freedom the woman who is walking in fear is not walking in her freedom, the woman who harbors unforgiveness in any area of your life is not walking in your freedom the woman who continues to walk in the same sinful patterns is not walking in your freedom, so here is the truth I've struggled with all these issues and I can tell you one thing for sure God was not pleased with me my actions but he remained faithful loving and forgiving, admitting was hard to see; it was not until I truly repented to God. I can remember till this day hearing god whisper that he loves me I am and that forgiven, and all those things were all gone, I no longer walk masked up and in bondage and God gets all the glory. Sisters great is Gods tender mercies towards you, there is no reason for anyone to stay bound God is forever faithful towards you. Great is God's grace. So, what do you do?

become women unmasked, you trust God; you must make radical steps to declare your DECLARATION OF DEPENDENCE. Yep, you read that correct GIVE GOD A YES! You must come to that place in your life where you affirm your dependence of Jesus. Jesus himself says that there is more that needs from thee; dependence declares that you cannot fix yourself that you cannot overcome your struggles or your hurt nor any unforgiveness on your own. You cannot even earn your way into grace. You NEED JESUS. You must declare that Jesus and only Jesus brings about your freedom your liberation identifying your own freedom is found in knowing and resting upon the fact that Jesus Christ truly is within you and that you must be in him no matter who or what you are, that JESUS is empowering and defending you in all things. Sister friend YOU HAVE BEEN REDEEMED SO SAY SO DECLARE YOUR INDEPENDENCE. TRUST GOD TO GET YOU TO THAT PLACE OF FREEDOM

CHAPTER 5 DRESSED TO A TEA

This is a mash up of two phrases describing perfection(dressed)well dressed in diligence. Colossians 3:12(KJV)therefore as God's chosen ones holy and beloved clothe yourselves with compassion, kindness, humility, meekness, and patience. Both Paul and Peter understand the act of dressing oneself as more than skin -

deep(1peter5:5) my sisters I know we all love a

good outfit I love clothes always have and always

will that be just facts. But I have learned that

those threads those garments they are merely

rags that cover you as an earthen vessel I have

discovered that as much as you are concerned

about how your outer appearance look and is

adorned that you must put forth all the effort in

order for you to win the spiritual war and to

operate effectively as a daughter of the king in

every aspect of your life you must on a daily

make sure that you are adorned in CHRIST WAR

CLOTHES . IT IS IMPORTANT to be mindful of how

you are dressing yourselves spiritually so that you

can face the enemy confidently and victoriously

by the grace and your faith in God. Ephesians 6

finally my brethren be strong in the lord and in the

power of his might put on the whole amour of God that we may be able to stand against the wiles of the devil. You are to make sure that as kingdom women you walk as a disciple properly attired so that you will be effective in all the areas of your life. Dressed for battle and dressed for success as powerful praying women leading your families your ministries and your communities and influencing those whom God has entrusted to you daily. A woman that spends time in prayer and in the presence of God is a powerful woman and a threat to Satan and all his schemes. Every day you must follow the path to equipping and adorning yourself properly in the things of God to walk as an effective woman. You must simply not just look the part of having a well-groomed well put together outer appearance and lack substance; hear this well .make sure you are making every effort to submit to the holy spirit so that he may expose your souls, your hearts , your minds too you in order that you may be dressed to a tea on the inside as well as the outside. You must develop a consistent prayer life being intentional in making sure that your heavenly father knows that you want to become closer to him you must ask God to draw you closer to him by opening your hearts to him. Girl you better check Gods reviews. God gets that credit; he blows my mind. We must practice humility daily we must ask God to revive and refresh your spirits clear your vision that you may begin to shine how he intended, you must commit to walking closely with God at all costs. As women we must be spiritually fit just as we like to get in the exercise to get into that outfit for an occasion that is how the exercise of a devoted prayer life will sustain you and strengthen your faith, you must approach God boldly with confidence.

1. Intimacy with God: embrace an intimate relationship with God pray about areas where you want to improve your connection with him.

2. Self -reflection: in the solitude of prayer Christian women confront our vulnerabilities and insecurities this process helps us appear stronger more resilient and compassionate.

3. Stress relief: prayer releases stress and brings a peace of mind. It allows you to communicate directly with your creator sharing your heart seeking guidance and expressing gratitude. Persistent prayer not only moves Gods hand, but it

prepares our hearts to recognize his

touch. The prayer of a righteous person is

as powerful and effective.

(james5:16Bniv)

PHILIPPIANS 3:14

I PRESS TOWARD THE MARK FOR THE PRIZE OF

THE HIGHER CALLING OF GOD IN CHRIST JESUS.

GOD IS CALLING you and it is imperative you

MUST ANSWER MY DEEPEST HEART DESIRE IS

THAT GOD USES ME GLOBALLY TO HELP BRING

WOMEN TO THEIR FULLEST GOD ORDAINED

POTENTIAL AND GOD ORDAINDED PURPOSE IN

CHRIST JESUS.

SO, AS I CONTINUE TO GOSSIP GIRL MAY YOUR

HEARTS BE OPENED AND ENLIGHTENED BY THE

UNCOMPROMISED WORD OF GOD REMEMBER

GOD HAS MADE YOU AN INSTRUMENT TO DO

HIS WORK AND SPEAK OUT FOR HIM. ITS TIME

TO TELL OTHERS OF THE NIGHT AND DAY

DIFFERENCE GOD HAS MADE FOR YOU FROM

NOTHING TO SOMETHING FROM REJECTED TO

ACCEPTED YOU ARE CALLED AND

ACCOUNTABLE.

SO, AS YOU GOSSIP GIRL KEEP IT

INTENTIONALLY ABOUT CHRIST.

CHAPTER 6 CONFESSIONS OF A CALL GIRL

We are to carry the glory of God. You are created

to call on the name Jesus.

(Jeremiah 33:3ESV) CALL TO ME AND I WILL

ANSWER YOU AND WILL TELL YOU GREAT AND

HIDDEN THINGS THAT YOU HAVE KNOWN

Luke 1:38 then Mary said here I am the servant of

the lord let it be with me according to your word

sister friend to be kept by God is when you call

upon him blessed is she who has believed that

what the lord has said to her will be

accomplished (luke1:45) a strong woman knows

that her power comes from God. A Godly woman

faithfully seeks God in everything that she does

(1Chronicles16:11) she is compassionate kind

and brave- a woman after Gods own heart

(1Samuel13:14) There is a divine calling that's

been planted within you that nagging persistent

feeling that there is some big purpose that you

are meant to do THAT GIRLFRIEND IS YOUR CALL

TO STEP INTO YOUR PURPOSE.

EPHESIANS 2:10

For WE ARE GODS' HANDIWORK CREATED

CHRIST JESUS TO DO GOOD WORKS WHICH

GOD PREPARED IN ADVANCE FOR US TO

DOCATCH THAT NOW! YOU WERE CREATED FOR

PURPOSE HERE ARE SOM EMPOWEREING

PUROSE DRIVEN SCRIPTURES FOR CALLED

WOMEN LIKE YOU. GOD IS CALLING you

EMBRACE YOUR GOD GIVEN CALLING.

SHE IS CLOTHED WITH STRENGHT AND DIGNITY

AND SHE LAUGHS WITHOUT FEAR OF THE

FUTURE. -PROVERBS31: twenty-five

GOD IS WITHIN HER, SHE WILL NOT FALL -

PROVERBS 46:5

AND WHO KNOWS BUT THAT YOU HAVE COME

TO YOUR ROYAL POSITION FOR SUCH A TIME AS

THIS -ESTHER 4:14

BUCKLE UP SWEETIE I KNOW THAT YOU ARE

INTRIGUED, EXCITED AND READY TO ANSWER

YOUR CALL AND STEP INTO YOUR DESTINY

REMEMBER ITS NOT ABOUT HAVING IT ALL

FIGURED OUT ITS ABOUT TRUSTING THAT THE

ONE WHO CALLED YOU IS FAITHFUL TO

ACCOMPLISH WHAT HE INTENDED FOR YOU.

THROUGHOUT THE BIBLE WOMEN HAVE BEEN

CALLED. TRUST GODS' FAITHFULNESS AS YOU

PURSUE YOUR CALLING AND GODS

COMMISSION.

TRUST IN THE LORD WITH ALL YOUR HEART AND

LEAN NOT ON YOUR OWN UNDERSTANDING

(proverbs 3:5)

Remember you can call on the lord and rest

assured that he will answer keep pushing

forward, remember even the trials are a part of

your journey but with God you got this.

Romans 8:28

And we know that in all things God works for the good of those who love him who have been called according to his purpose.

Allow God to make you over again. God made to shine God will create in you a clean heart and create the right spirit within you.

WE ARE GODS' MASTERPIECE (EPHESIANS 2:20)

REMINDERS:

1. VALUABLE

2. CREATED AS BELOVED WITH CHRIST

3. BEAUTIFUL

AFFIRMATIONS FROM THE BIBLE:

God is my strength and my shield -psalms 27.7.

I will not be moved -Psalms125:1

The lord will fight for me- exodus 14:14

I was created for such a time as this-Esther 4:14

I am more than a conqueror through him that

loves me-Romans 8:37

I can do all things through Christ Jesus who

strengthens me- Philippians 4:13

God has given me power love and a sound mind-2

Timothy 1:7

The lord is my light and my salvation of whom

shall, I fear.

The lord is the strength of my life of whom shall I

be afraid-Psalms27:1

The lord is my rock and my fortress and my

deliverer-Psalms18:2

If God is for me who can be against me-Romas

8:31.

I am strong and courageous my god is with me-

Joshua 1:9

No weapon formed against shall prosper and

every tongue.

That rises against you in judgement you shall

condemn this is the heritage of the servants of the

lord and their righteousness is of me saith the

lord-Isaiah 54:17

I will not fear my god is with me-Isaiah 41:10

I AM ENOUGH-2 CORINTHIANS 12:9

BUT HE WAS WOUNDED FOR OUR

TRANSGRESSIONS HE WAS BRUISED FOR OUR

INIQUITIES

THE CHASTISEMENT OF OUR PEACE WAS UPON

HIM AND WITH HIS STRIPES WE ARE HEALED-

ISAISH 53:5

And trusting God, we can be kept Gods plan has been my secret to being kept my sisters, it is about your relationship with Him. GOD, I LOVE YOU SO MUCH FOR LOVING ME SO MUCH EVEN WHEN I REFUSED TO LOVE MYSELF... BUT GOD. YOUR MERCY KEPT ME SO I WOULDN'T LET GO....

CHAPTER 7 YOU GOT IT GIRL

And the angel came in unto her, and said, hail, though that are highly favored, the lord is with thee: blessed art though among women. And when she saw him, she was troubled at his saying and cast in her mind what manner of salutation this should be. And the angel said unto her, fear

not thou hast Favor with GOD. (LUKE 1:28-30).

Sis be encouraged that God will supply every one

of your needs so let me encourage to only speak

blessings over your life. God is taking all your

issues and turning them into opportunities. You

are fabulous in every way, which is the way that

the expert builder designed you from the

beginning. God said in the beginning that

everything he made was good before the fall of

Adam, and after that he supplied the perfect

substitution Jesus Christ for you so that you could

get right back into the proper position, now it's up

to you if you are going to walk as if you really to

have the Favor of God all over you. I encourage

you to be beautiful and be you. There is

absolutely no substitution or additives that you

can take to try to make sure self-perfect, its only

by God's grace and the pouring of GODS love on

you that can fill every void that you have. BE you

sis because everyone else is taken, be you sis

because the blessings that GOD HAS FOR YOU IS

FOR YOU. GOD CAN NOT BLESS WHO YOU

PRETEND TO BE, SEE IN GODS WORD IF

CLEARLY SAID YOU THOU ART BLESSED AND

HIGHLY FAVORED. The enemy cannot take away

the promises of God but if he can discourage you

to the point that you stop believing Gods word

and Gods purpose for you, then that is when you

will begin that doubt that you are favored. You

must let the devil know that you are encouraged,

and you must also encourage another sister and

remind her to that no matter what is going on that

she must stay strong and that she has the favor of

God on her life. Girl you got it that trial you are

going through as major as it me appear it is just FEAR and FEAR has been deemed as FALSE EVIDENCE APPEARING REAL... GIRL LOOK I CALL myself A BIGSTUFFMAGNET THE FAVOR OF GOD IS ALL OVER ME, I DO NOT BELIEVE IN worshipping the starts and the moons or the universe But I do honor adore and worship the CREATOR OF ALL THOSE THINGS... I ACKNOWLEDGE HIS SOVEREIGNTY, HIS SPLENDOR AND HIS MAJESTY, GOD IS MY LAW OF ATTRACTION. THE FAVOR OF GOD WILL cause the right things to be attracted to you. Girl you better recognize the power that you own and that is the word of God; you got it girl. Matthew 6:33 but look for first the kingdom of God and his righteousness and all these things will be added to you. Girl, you got you better begin to pray like you know it.

DECLARE THIS:

1.The pressures of life will not defeat you

2.confusion will not discourage you

3.oppostion will not deter you

4.hard hits will not destroy you.

You got it GIRL. DO NOT GIVE UP ON WHAT GOD
HAS PROMISED YOU. Embrace your reward of
favor and keep your mind and thoughts positive
because your thoughts set the course of your
destiny. Renew your mind often a renewed mind
is the link to experiencing the power of living a
transformed life. You must cast down every
thought in your mind that does not align to gods
perfect design for your destiny and Sis in order for
you to know that design you to read study and

meditate on the word of God often, make sure that you are surrounding yourself with purpose pushers and not dream killers or character assassinators; Get you some sister friends who will celebrate your favor and your wins in life, and also correct you when you are stepping out of alignment with the Gods plan. Do not be scared to shift when God says that season is over. Some people are not meant to go with you to your next, you do not have to forget them but do not miss the shift because of them. Girl the favor of God will cause you to get to altitudes; remain humble never move yourself out of a servant's position, Jesus calls you to a lower altitude then you will start to have the right attitude.

Chapter 8 The Rules of Engagement

And when you pray, do not be like the hypocrites for they love to pray standing in the synagogues and on the street corners to be seen by others truly I tell you they have received their reward in full. But when you pray go into your room close the door and pray to our father who is unseen then your father who sees what is done in secret will reward. (Matthew 6:5-7)

Sis make sure are mastering the rules of engagement. Prayer is speaking to God, Girl you best learn how to stop praying to be spiritual and learn how to pray to be powerful; to be used by God has a force on in spirit realm to be a sharpshooter right her on earth. From your mouth to Gods ears in the name of Jesus should always be your declaration when you open your mouth to communicate with God. Jesus teaches the disciples how to pray and not once models a two-way approach prayer is speaking to God. Prayer is your conversation with God rather than talking to about your cares to everybody else. God has selected you as one of his official legislators and law enforcement against, you are important sis, you must realize that you are to effect and enforce Gods original plans and purposes and the plans of Satan. God has given you permission in scripture to boldly come before him and bring your needs to him. A prayer strategy is simply the combination of those needs and the scripture god has given you to lean on while you present them to him.

Here are five simple steps of a prayer strategy.

1.you cannot be a sis who quit. you must remain persistent with your prayers.

2.you must feed your faith by bringing your request to God tell your request to God.

3.stay standing on your God's word keep your eyes on the next step of obedience instead of on the outcome you wish, god's outcome may not always be what we expect.

4.trust that gods timing is perfect, and his answer is coming, your confidence comes in trusting that God is coming

5.god is faithful god is god gods timing is different than yours trust that he is working it out. Trust that you are not forgotten.

Sis Make sure that you open yourself up to God in prayer by telling him how you feel and what you are experiencing. You can also thank God for the things he has one in your life. sis prayer is more than just a list of requests, it is a conversation with God. Make sure you are meditating on God's word and listening to his voice can help you get to know him and yourself. You can as God to speak to you through the holy spirit as you read the bible. Sis keeps you a journal or paper to write down anything you think God might be saying. God will often speak to you way you will understand by shifting and directing your thoughts. It is so important that you pray to God with passion, prayers should flow from your heart to gods with enthusiastic emotion. SIS MAKE SURE YOU ARE USING THE ACTS MODELWHEN YPU ARE PRAYING: WHICH STANDS FOR ADORATION, CONFESSION, to him. AND SUPPLICATION. ASLO SUREENDER. ACKNOWLEDGE A NEED/PROBLEM.BE CONFIDENT That GOD IS YOUR

SOLUTION.KNOW THAT YOU HAVE THE ABILITY TO STAND ON SCRIPTURE.PERSISTANCE IS KEY SIS. A STRATEGIC PRAYER LIFE IS a result of living in the intimacy with the father listening following trusting and obeying. Sis, you have a purpose like Jesus. Looking for and saving the lost and destroying the works of the enemy. You cannot do that without the same position of love, power and the same kind of prayers that are the bible. You must let go of traditions and embrace scripture and God. Sis it is time you change your perspective and see from a different position, get yourself in a prayer position Sis. When you put God first, he will cover the rest, so remember his will. God has given you permission sis to boldly come before him and bring your needs. So, to all my Gossip Girls this session has been great, I am so Glad that God allowed me to share this conversation piece with you, I am also honored to introduce me to me. NO MORE PIECES, LET ME INTRODUCE THE WHOLE VERSION OF ME. I LOVE YOU ALL ON PURPOSE AND THERE IS ABSOLUTELY NOTHING YOU CAN DO ABOUT IT. IM EXPECTING TO SEE YOU ALL SOON IN A CITY SOMWHERE SO GET READY TO GOSSIP GIRL.

Chapter 9 KEEP WALKING

SIS, I PROMISE YOU THAT WHEREVER YOU WALK; YOU WILL NOT WALK ALONE. GOD WILL WALK WITH UOU THROUGH EVERY TRIAL, THROUGH EVERY TEMPTATION AND EVERY PROBLEM. NOT ONLY WILL GOD STRENTHGEN YOU THROUGH THE JOURNEY HIS PRESENCE

WILL BE WITH UOU AND YOU WILL NOT LOOK
LIKE WHAT YOU HAVE GONE THROUGH ONCE
YOU COME OUT ON THE OTHER SIDE OF
THROUGH. JUST LIKE THE THREE HEBREW BOYS
WERE CAST IN THE MIDST OF THE FIRE, AND
THEY HAD NO HURT GOD WILL CAUSE YOU TO
WALK IN THE FURNACE THAT WAS DESIGNED TO
KNOCK YOY OFF OF YOUR FEET , GOD WILL
EVEN CAUSE YOU TO NOT LOOSE YOUR
BALANCE WHEN YOU HAVE TO WALK THE PATHS
OF DIFFICULTIES IN LIFE; YOU CAN REST
ASSURED THAT GOD WILL CONTINUE TO ORDER
YOUR STEPS. EVERY LITTLE STEP YOU TAKE GOD
WILL BE RIGHT THERE WITH YOU.

 IT IS AMAZING HOW GOD WILL ALLOW TO EVEN
WALL THROUGH THE VALLEY OF THE SHALLOW
OF DEATH THAT WAS DESIGNED TO TRIP YOU UP

AND TRIP YOU OUT.GOD WITH IS STRATEGIC

SELF WITH THE ASSITANCE OF THE HOLY SPIRIT

AS YOUR PERSONAL GPS WILL HELP YOU WALK

PASS YOUR ENEMIES ;THAT WERE PUT IN

POSITION TO HINDER YOUR ASSIGNTMENT, GIRL

ITS FUNNY HOW GOD WILL USE THEM AS A MILE

MARKER TO MAKE SURE THAT YOU KNOW THAT

YOU ARE ON THE RIGHT DESTINATION, RIGHT

ON TARGET JUST KEEP YOUR FOCUS ON GOD

AND CONTINUE TO WALK. OFTEN TIME THE

ENEMY DOES NOT HAVE TO KILL YOUR PURPOSE

WHILE YOU ARE ON YOUR JOURNEY; HE ONLY

WANTS TO GET YOU DISTRACTED; SO, YOU CAN

STOP WALKING. THIS IS WHY PAUL SAID IN

EPHESIANS 5:15 SEE THEN THAT YE WALK

CIRCUMSPECTLY NOT AS FOOLS BUT AS WISE.

WALK CAREFULLY AND WATCH WHERE YOU ARE

GOING THE ENEMY WOULD LOVE TO PLACE

OBSTACKLES IN YOUR PATHTHAT WOULD
CAUSE YOU TO QUIT, SO WATCH WHERE YOU
ARE GOING. I NEVER UNDERSTOOD ALL THE
TIME WHERE I WAS GOING OR WHERE GOD WAS
TAKING ME BUT I JUST KEPT ON WALKING.GOD
PROMISE YOU THAT YOU MAY EVEN HAVE TO
CRY SOMETIMES AS YOU WALK THROUGH LIFES
JOURNIES, BUT TEARS ARE OKAY: HE ASSURED
YOU THAT WEEPING MAY ENDURE FOR BUT A
NIGHT BUT JOY COMETH IN THE MORNING. SIS
YOU ARE A KINGDOM WOMAN AND YOU MUST
DECLARE THAT YOU ARE GONNA WALK IN THE
WAY OF A KINGDOM WOMAN AND BELIEVE THAT
YOU WILL DISCOVER YOUR TRUE SPIRITUAL
DESTINY AND YOUR LIFE AND THE LIVES OF
THOSE YOU ENCOUNTER WILL BE
TRANSFORMED.

5 WAYS A WISE WOMAN WALKS WITH GOD

1.HUMBLY

2.BY FAITH

3.IN THE SPIRIT

4.IN LIGHT

5.IN GOOD WORKS.

SIS GOD ALSO WANTS YOU TO KNOW WHERE

HE IS TAKING YOU. GOD WANTS YOU TO TAKE

THE FIRST STEP AND MAKE SURE YOU ARE

HELPING AND ENCOURAGING OTHER SISTERS

AND STRENGHTENING THEM, AS HE EQUIPS

YOU, HE WANTS YOU TO EQUIP OTHERS AND

HELP THEM GROW THEIR WALK WITH THE LORD.

A WOMAN WHO WALKS WITH GOD WILL

ALWAYS REACH HER DESTINATION.SIS IT IS VERY IMPORTANT THAT YOU BE CONSISTENTIN YOUR WALK WITH GOD.CONSISTENCY IN YOUR DAILY WALK WITH GOD MAKES YOUR LIFE EASY, IT MAKES YOU A STRONG WOMEN; BATTLE READY.WALKING WITH GOD HELPS YOU ADPOT A GODLY LIFESTYLE, MEDITATING ON GOD DAILYAND LIVING YOUR LIFE ACCORDING TO HIS WILL. SIS IS GOOD TO KNOW GODS' GOODNESS AND THE BLESSINGSHAS BESTOWED ON YOU.

IT IS SO IMPORTANT THAT YOU WALK IN IN LOVE AS SISTERS OF CHRIST, AND ALSO WALK WORTHY AS A BELIEVINGWOMEN IN FELLOWSHIP WITH EACH OTHER. IN JUDGES 21:21 THE DAUGHTERS OF SHILOH WHEN THE TABERNACLE IN THE DAYS OF THE JUDGES WAS

PITCHED AT SHILOH. A GROUP OF YOUNG GIRLS WOULD CELEBRATE GODS' GOODNESS AND PRAISE GOD AND EXPRESS JOY IN GOD. THEY WOULD COME AND THEY WOULD ASSENBLE AT THE TABERNACLE.

AS WOMEN GOD HAS GIVEN YOU A SPECIFIC GIFTS, GOD REALLY DID CREATE US MY SISTERS TO WALK IN UNITY AND NOT IN DIVISION, JEALOUSNESS, OR TO BE ENVIOUS OF ONE ANOTHER. GOD CREATED YOU SIS TO BE A BUILDER. YOU HAVE BEEN GIVEN AUTHORITY TO DECLARE GODS' DIVINE TRUTH WITH HOLY SPIRIT FUELED POWER. IT IS TIME THAT YOU BEGIN TO SPEAK SPIRIYUAL AUTHORITY OVER YOURSELF AND YOUR FAMILY

MAKE SURE THAT YOU ARE WALKING AS A WOMAN OF PRAYER, PURPOSE, AND PASSION. SIS, YOU HAVE WORTH, YOU HAVE PURPOSE AND NO MATTER WHERE YOU ARE IN YOUR PRESENT SITUATION IN LIFE, YOU ARE WOMAN OF VALUE, HOPE, AND EXCELLENCE. SIS YOU SHOULD BE B DISPLAYING THE FRUIT OF THE SPIRIT GIVEN IN GALATIANS 6: LOVE, JOY, PEACE, PATIENCE, GENTLENESS, AND SELF-CONTROL. GIRL NO, YOU DO WILL NOT POSSESS THES QUALITIES PERFECTLY, YOU MUST AND WILL CONTINUALLY GROW IN THEM AS A RESULT OF THE HOLY SPIRITS WORK IN YOU.SIS I NEED YOU STAND UP AND EMBRACE YOUR GOD GIVEN IDENTITY AND PURPOSE. YOU ARE QUEEN, LIVE THE BEST VERSION OF YOURSELF. YOU ARE DAUGHTER OF GODS KINGDOM; YOU HAVE BEEN BORN AGAIN.

CHANGED FROM A CARNAL AND FALLEN STATE TO A STATE OF RIGHTEOUSNESS. SIS YOU ARE AUTHENTIC, ETHICAL, PEACEMAKER, AND YOU ARE JOYFUL EVEN WHEN PERSECUTED. MY SISTER, I CHALLENGE YOU TO RISE UP TO THE OCCASION AND BE A FAITHFUL FRIEND, GIRL YOU BETTER WALK LIKE RUTH DID.YOU NEED TO BE A WOMEN WHO HEAR AND KEEP THE WORD OF GOD RATHER THAN A WOMEN WHO CHASE THE THINGS OF THE WORLD. I BECAME FREE WHEN I POSITIONED MYSELF AND BEGAN TO OPERATE UNDER THE AUTHORITY OF GOD. I FOUND POWER AND PURPOSE, WHEN I SURRENDERED MY ALL TO GOD. GODS PURPOSE DETERMINES YOUR DESIGN SIS.

My deepest heart desire is that God uses me to be an effective witness here earth to help restore broken women into beautiful butterflies. Sisters

God loves you; flaws and all. God is waiting on

you to step into your divine assignments;

everything that you need God has already placed

it on the inside of you. Remember you must walk

in faith to walk in the fullness that God wants for

you. Sometimes bad outcomes will push you to

your next outcome. God has designed you to

succeed, my encouragement is that you get in the

proper position and posture.

A Purpose Prayer: God, empower me to make the

spiritual and personal transformation to prepare

to walk in my calling, and to move forward in what

I am ready to do. Father, fill me with confidence

based in who You are and help me to trust you

with the outcome so I can have courage to step

out into what You are calling me to do In Jesus

name, Amen.

Psalms 34:8

Gossip Girl

Tywanda Marie' Jones

This book is in Memory of my Darling Son, My

Angel

Trent Matthew Jones 12/21/20-5/13/2020

Baby boy "JETT" I could not understand why you.

Always was on the Go there. God blessed me with

you for eighteen sweet years that was very

impactful to me, dad , to your siblings and each

individual that your path crossed I can remember

one of your basketball coaches told me that the

skills you possessed in that sport was from God, I

also remember you tearing your meniscus and

you refused to accept that diagnosis because you wanted to play football that Friday and you said momma didn't you tell me that God gave me the power to lay hands in the name of Jesus and I can be Healed. And my GOD you believed that son and did just that and you did not have that surgery. at the age of fourteen God spoke to

Me that you were a profit and that your life would have me travel around.

The world, My God so as you strengthen me daily to continue to fulfill your promise to me even now.

God, you get the Glory. THERE IS LIFE AFTER DEATH

And to my Mommy

Linda McClay Mosby 11/5/1950-July/21/2021

Momma you told me you would love me until

Your last breath and my God in Heaven you

Did just that...We talked daily so until we meet

again. FLY HIGH SWEET LYNN YOU BYPASSED

COMPTON CALIFORNIA AND TOOK FLIGHT

#955 ALL THE WAY TO HEAVEN.

I love and miss you both immensely, But OH TO

BE KEPT BY JESUS

TO MY FOUR LIVING HEARTBEATS, I LOVE YOU

ALL SO EXTREMELY BUNCHES AND BUNCHES

AND BUNCHES AND BUNCHES. TREVAR,

TATYANNA, TIA, AND TYRA Thanks for loving me.

WE HAVE GROWN THROUGH SO MUCH

TOGETHER; DETOURS, REROUTES, DELAYS

DENIALS OH BUT WE ARE KEPT BY THE GRACE

AND MERCIES OF OUR LORD AND SAVIOR.

BABIES OUR LATTER SHALL BE GREATER... IN MY

LIL BOOSIE VOICE GOD WILL ALLOW US TO

SHOW THE WORLD. My prayer is that my Faith is

meeting Gods plan for Us. Faith is meeting Gods

plan for Us. To Charles, Chris, Curtis, Quentin

and Wilford growing with five guys really spoiled

me to this day My continued prayer is that God

continue to BLESS KEEP AND PROSPER and

perfect all things pertaining to you all I love you

all.

BISHOP RONALD C. JOHNSON and LADY NINA

JOHNSON WORDS WILL NEVER BE ABLE TO

EXPRESS THE SENTIMENTS OF MY HEART

TOWARDS YOU both AS MY OVERSEERS AND

SPIRITUAL PARENTS, CONFIDENTS, YOU BOTH

STRETCH ME TO NOT BE SCARED OF THE

KINGDOM ASSIGNMENTS GOD HAS SET BEFORE

ME. BISHOP!!!!! NINTA!!! I LOVE YOU BOTH SO
MUCH. BISHOP I WILL NEVER

FORGET THAT WENDESDAY NIGHT TEN YEARS
AGO WHEN YOU ENTERED THE SANCTUARY
WITH URGENCY I WAS ON THE FOURTH PEW ON
THE RIGHT SIDE OF THE SANCTUARY PRAYING
AND YOU GENLTY TAPPED MY Shoulder SAYING
MINISTER TEE; GOD SAID ITS TIME FOR YOUR
WORD; MY GOD AND EVEN WHEN I RAN YOU
YET STILL TRUSTED GOD FOR THAT WORD HE
GAVE YOU ABOUT ME. BISHOP I HONOR THE
GOD IN YOU AND THE GIFTINGS OF THE MANTLE
THAT'S UPON YOU... LADY NINA GREAT IS THY
FAIHTHFULNESS.YOU ARE WISE AND HUMBLE.
WE ARE GONNA KEEP EXPECTING THE
MANIFESTATIONS OF GOD AND THANK YOU FOR
LOVING AND COVERING MY BISHOP.

PASTOR CHRIS DAWSON BUTLER, OH MY HOW

YOUR MINISTER TY LOVES YOU.THANKS FOR

ALWAYS POURING INTO ME CORRECTING ME

WHEN I NEED CORRECTION. I APPRECIATE

YOUR Authenticity AND MY SAFE PLACE WITH

YOU. I KNOW MY MOM IS AT PEACE. YOU ARE

TRUE JEWEL. CONSISTENT IN ALL YOU DO.

BABY IM SO BLESSED TO HAVE PURPOSE

PUSHERS THAT PRAY PERSISTANT AND EXPECT

THE MANIFESTATIONS OF GOD WITH ME!

MR. AND MRS CARLTON and Odester Ann HARRIS all I can say is that it is a blessing to be a blessing THEY ARE TRULY GODS APPOINTED ELDERS.... I PRAY GOD CONTINUES TO ALLOW YOU BOTH TO SEE WHAT HE SEES. Much love.

Mr. and Mrs. Ameer and Vanessa Saleem, Great is thy faithfulness to all my visions. God Jewels keep occupying and advancing the kingdom right here on earth I love you all.

To My Uncle James McClay thanks for being not only my uncle but for being my father you made sure that I never went without anything and you made sure I saw something other than Plaquemine growing up; I thought you were harsh growing up; But God I'm so grateful for your teachings and the structure. Pastor Ricardo Handy Sr. and Lady Latoya Handy I am so grateful for you both on my journey, Thanks for instilling in me to always work from a spirit of excellency in everything that I do and to always build my faith and my family. I love you both.

EVANGELIST BRIDGET RENEE SCOTT, KAMISHA HALL THOMPSON Thank you for being consistent with me Lord I'm so grateful for our relationships my dear FRIENDS LORD JESUS GLORY Hallelujah. I LOVE YOU AND THERE IS ABSOLUTELY NOTHING YOU CAN. DO ABOUT IT.... Reverand George and Lady Amanda Barrett THANKS FOR BEING TRUE GENUINE FRIENDS. I love you both dearly.

GOD, I THANK YOU FOR HELPING ME TO SEE ME

THE WAY, THAT YOU SEE ME.... ... GOD, I

PROMISE TO LIVE MY LIFE LIKE A BLIND MAN... I

CAN'T SEE IT... BUT I BELIEVE. ONLY BLINDED

EYES CAN SEES. IT IS WORKING OUT FOR ME. I

WILL LIVE AGAIN. THANK YOU, TAMELA MANN,

FOR BLESSING MY LIFE WITH THIS

DECLARATION... ITS WORKING FOR ME....

THE END BY THE GRACE OF GOD

MINISTER TYWANDA JONES

THE APOSTOLIC SPIRITUAL MIDWIFE

Made in the USA
Columbia, SC
29 October 2024

45011426R00046